IRRITATION

THE DESTRUCTIVE FIRE

Torkom Saraydarian

Aquarian Educational Group
P.O. Box 267
Sedona, AZ 86336

ABOUT THE AUTHOR

Torkom Saraydarian was born in Asia Minor. Since childhood he has tried to understand the mystery called man.

He visited monasteries, ancient temples, and mystery schools in order to find the answers to his burning questions.

He lived with Sufis, dervishes, Christian mystics, and masters of temple music and dance. It took long years of discipline and sacrifice to absorb the Ageless Wisdom from its true sources. Meditation became a part of his daily life, and service a natural expression of his soul.

Torkom Saraydarian is the author of forty books, which are read throughout the world. They have been translated into German, Dutch, Danish, Portuguese, French, Spanish, Italian, and Greek. He has lectured in many cities; he has written numerous articles for philosophical and religious publications.

He is a violinist, pianist, composer, teacher, lecturer, mechanical engineer, meteorologist, writer, and philosopher.

Note: Suggestions here given about using oils and doing exercises are given as guidelines. They should be used with discretion and after receiving professional advice.

©1983 by Torkom Saraydarian
All Rights Reserved
Second Printing 1991

No part of this publication may be reproduced, stored in a retrieval system, or transmitted in any form, by any means, electronic, mechanical, photocopying, recording or otherwise, without permission in writing from the copyright owner or his representatives.

ISBN: 0911794-17-4
Library of Congress No.: 91-076088

Printed in the United States of America

Other Books by Torkom Saraydarian

The Ageless Wisdom
The Bhagavad Gita
Breakthrough to Higher Psychism
Challenge for Discipleship
Christ, The Avatar of Sacrificial Love
A Commentary on Psychic Energy
Cosmic Shocks
Cosmos in Man
Dialogue With Christ
Earthquakes and Disasters
Flame of Beauty, Culture, Love, Joy
Hiawatha and the Great Peace
The Hidden Glory of the Inner Man
I Was
Joy and Healing
Legend of Shamballa
Other Worlds
The Psyche and Psychism
The Psychology of Cooperation and Group Consciousness
The Purpose of Life
The Science of Becoming Oneself
The Science of Meditation
The Sense of Responsibility in Society
Sex, Family, and the Woman in Society
The Solar Angel
Spiritual Regeneration
The Spring of Prosperity
Symphony of the Zodiac
Talks on Agni
Triangles of Fire
Unusual Court
Woman, Torch of the Future
The Year 2000 & After

There are many causes of disease, but there is a cause which is not sufficiently emphasized, explained, and publicized. This source of disease is everywhere; it hides in many forms and enters into our system with various logical excuses. This cause is called irritation. Let us see what the causes of irritation are:

1. agitation of the astral body
2. stress of temper
3. hatred, dislike, prejudice, continuous rejection of a person, group or idea
4. a sense of being abused or a sense of being deceived or exploited
5. reaction to things which do not agree with one's own way of doing things — resentment
6. thoughts of revenge or plans of destruction
7. complaining
8. self-interest, self-sufficiency, and self-satisfaction
9. criticism, gossip, quarreling
10. ingratitude
11. demanding, forcing, intolerance
12. inferiority complex
13. impatience and hurry

14. conscious distortion of facts
15. intensification of the astral body
16. noise

The result of irritation is the production of a poison which is called *imperil* by Master Morya. Imperil is a spreading poison which slowly descends upon our nervous system as we burn our etheric and astral bodies through irritation. Imperil cuts off the channels of electricity which flow through the network of our nervous system. This poison continuously spreads when it is fed. Once the electrical system of the body is blocked in various places and the electricity is hampered or cut, serious physical and psychological problems spread their roots into our nature.

If the electricity coming from the etheric body, from the astral and mental centers, and from the transpersonal center within man is impeded, those organs which do not receive enough electricity develop malfunctions. They become retarded, they slow down, and eventually heavy apathy sets in, thus turning the glands and organs into a hotbed for germs and microbes.

In other cases, when the cells have excess energy to fight, they become panicky and overactive, and they develop tumors and cancers. Imperil can spread itself or come into existence in any of the vehicles of the personality, eventually manifesting as psychological and physical diseases. The poison most often accumulates around the area of the solar plexus, and causes complications and troubles in the digestive system. Then it spreads to the whole nervous system and contaminates the aura of the person.

Irritation and imperil do not attack those whose consciousness is focused within their heart and head. Before the attack reaches them they can dissolve it through loving understanding. But if the focus of consciousness is in the emotional nature, and occupied with the interests of the lower centers, then imperil accumulates around the solar plexus and lowers the vitality of the man to such a degree that eventually the resistance of the body weakens and surrenders to various attacks of germs or diseases. Irritation causes inflammation in various organs of the body: in the nose, in the eyes, in the ears, or in the reproductive organs.

Let us explain the causes of irritation:

1. *Agitation of the astral body.* This can be caused in various ways, for example, watching a criminal movie, reading a book which speaks about disasters, crimes, or subjects which cause you to be worried, fearful, and depressed. Agitation of the astral body can be the result of intensive anger of one near you, or the result of verbal attacks. Many times our astral body is agitated when we lose the support on which we were leaning or were selfishly using.

2. *Stress of temper.* This is a phenomenon in which you use your willpower to reach your desires or to get people to do what you want. If they do not do what you want, you lose your temper and create abundant imperil in your system.

3. *Hatred, dislike, continuous rejection of a person, group or idea* produce irritation and imperil. They create agitation in your astral nature by the injection of negative ideas and negative feelings. Hatred continually obscures your vision and short-circuits your vital energy system.

Dislikes and rejections increase the poison of irritation to such a degree that the person loses all his magnetism on the three levels of personality and turns into an instrument of attack or isolation. Prejudice creates certain patterns of mental and emotional substance which cause irritation when confronted with expanding horizons or with new concepts. M.M. says, . . . *One cannot free oneself from irritation without uprooting prejudice.* . . .

Agni Yoga Society, *Agni Yoga*, para. 382.

Prejudice can be overcome through continuous expansion of consciousness and with sincere striving.

4. *Those who think that people are always taking advantage of them, that they are always deceived by people, or exploited by them,* create irritation in their system with the resultant imperil. People with such a psychology try to take revenge on those whom they think are taking advantage of them. Actions resulting from such a cause create further sources of irritation and imperil.

5. *Those who always want to see things done in their own way* cannot escape irritation when things are done some other way. Such people do not respect the freedom of others to do things in their own way. They are so attached to their own thoughtforms, to their habits and ways of activities that the slightest deviation by others from their own ways causes them feelings of loss and pain.

6. *Thoughts of revenge and plans of destruction* are a source of continuous irritation. Generations of people are poisoned by such a course of life. Their joy and happiness are taken away from them, and they are not able to adapt themselves to the requirements of the present situations of life. The past controls them in the present, and the present cannot see the future clearly because of their involvement in the past, and because of the feeling of revenge and expected reaction to their actions.

7. *Complaining* creates imperil. Complaining is emotional and mental friction. It takes away the magnetism

of man and fills his nature with imperil. Watch people who always complain. They develop various disorders and eventually are caught in serious health problems. A joyous and happy heart does not allow the formation of imperil.

8. *Self-interest, self-sufficiency, and self-satisfaction* are the most widespread diseases on our planet and are the sources of abundant irritation. The true course of evolution, the path of the heart, and the wisdom of the soul are against self-interest, against self-sufficiency, against self-satisfaction, but *for* inclusiveness, *for* givingness, and *for* group appreciation. Once the personality is charged with negativity, it creates frictions with the radiations of the higher natures, and the result is irritation.

9. *Criticism and gossip* are very common ways to produce irritation in oneself and others. Criticism agitates the emotional body, while gossip charges the astral body with negative polarization, creating irritation and imperil. One can observe easily how one feels weaker physically and mentally after a period of criticism or gossip. Actually, imperil is one of the greatest consumers of psychic energy; it almost devours it completely and depletes the whole human mechanism. On the other hand, appreciation, gratitude, loving understanding, and the spirit of encouragement uplift people and charge them with health-giving energies.

10. *Ingratitude* creates irritation. It is also a sign of being attacked by imperil. That is why sages warned us to stay away from ungrateful people because their poison may reach us and contaminate our aura.

11. *A demanding, forcing, intolerant spirit* will pay a very high price to gain health. A demand is an outgoing force which, when unfulfilled, bounces back and hits the originating source. Forcefulness is imposition of one's own

will on others. Others have their own will. The clash causes irritation, especially when one fails to subdue others. Intolerance is a steady exercise of pressure of your will on others to stop the way they live, the way they feel, the way they think, and the way they worship. Intolerance always creates strong resistance, and causes heavy taxation through irritation.

12. *An inferiority complex* is another source of irritation. The person identifies with his failures and shortcomings, and assumes that others are more beautiful, more successful, more able, and greater than he is. He feels frustrated. He becomes rejective, critical, and tries to escape from people so as not to feel his inferiority or to recognize their superiority. This eventually leads him into irritation.

13. *Impatience and hurry* cause more sickness in the world than one can imagine. In impatience, our aura stretches itself out and takes on a distorted form. Thus the emotional body is agitated, causing irritation. Hurry puts great pressures on the astral and etheric bodies and on the nervous system, irritating them violently and producing imperil.

14. *Conscious distortion of facts* creates great tension in the astral and etheric bodies. In conscious distortion you are breaking the natural harmony of your energy system in your mental and emotional bodies. This creates a pressure which slowly grows, becomes fear and doubt, and then changes into irritation.

15. *Intensification of the astral body* is caused primarily by Hatha Yoga exercises, breathing exercises, chanting mantrams, doing Tai Chi, and, curiously enough, by excessive sexual activity. Some hallucinogenic drugs cause intensification. In addition, heavy intensification of the astral body is caused by disco music, rock music, acid

music, and the like. They produce heavy imperil. Accompanied by dancing, they almost paralyze the mental system and lead a person into moral and physical depletion.

 M.M., speaking about irritation, says, . . . *The emanations of irritation not only deny entrance to the thoughts We send, but even a touch is not to be sensed by the hedgehog.*
   Agni Yoga Society, *Leaves of Morya's Garden, Vol. I*, para. 249.

 16. *Noise* is another heavy factor causing irritation. Noise from airplanes or any other mechanical noise which strains the nerves and irritates them produces an abundance of imperil. It is known that among people who are living in noisy areas are found the most psychological problems, crimes, divorces, and suicides.

 Noise can be audible or inaudible. Audible noise is chaotic sound, sound which does not carry meaning, plan or purpose. Inaudible noise comes from ugly forms, inharmonious colors, radio waves, and electromagnetic storms. Curiously enough, inaudible noises are generated also from the chaotic thinking of people. Noise, in both forms, penetrates not only into our ears, but also into our subtle bodies and creates heavy disturbances which manifest as mental, emotional and etheric diseases, and physical illnesses.

 Protection from natural noise is possible to a certain degree if human understanding defeats human greed. For example, the noise of airplanes will have a detrimental effect on the genes of people and they will reproduce retarded children with many psychological turbulences. All this is a great burden for the rest of humanity.

 Many electric machines in our homes constantly bombard our subtle centers with noise, and we pay a great amount of money for their damage. Noise creates short circuits in the line of spiritual impression or inspiration. Great ideas cannot reach a man when he is full of irritation and imperil.

The Teaching advises that those who are leading groups, states, or nations live in areas where there is a minimum of noise. Decreasing noise pollution will bring greater health to nations and greater clarity of mind to those who are serving people in many ways. Ancient prophets who guided the evolution of races were dwellers of deserts, caves, and mountains.

Our decisions and plans will have greater divine inspiration if they are made in the silence of nature. We are told that one of the points of the Plan of the Great Ones is to decrease noise.

Noise has a disintegrative effect on the mind. Irritation emanates from our physical body as waves of distorted force, smell, odor, and perspiration. It builds a stagnated sphere around us, which prevents the waves of light and wisdom from reaching us and being registered by our heart and mind. Often an open or overactive solar plexus grasps such waves of light, and because of the heavy layers of imperil and irritation, distorts them and translates them through its wishful thinking into personal messages given by Great Ones. As these waves of messages are accumulated in the solar plexus, the solar plexus gets abnormally enlarged and transmits more energy than the organs below the diaphragm can assimilate. Coupled with imperil, this energy produces all the complaints a human being has in his organs below the diaphragm.

We are told that imperil accumulates in the walls of the nerve channels and slowly spreads throughout the entire organism. Astral currents, while passing through the nerve channels which are full of imperil, decompose and leave decomposed astral substance in these channels.

There is another poison which is created by

> *... The occurrences of disruption of the elements [which] give rise to a powerful poisonous gas. Usually this gas is easily assimilated in space, but the chemical rays of the sun are driving the gaseous waves into the layers near to the planet. ... Irritation and its offspring, imperil, combine easily with the poison of space, which is called 'aeroperil'....*
> Agni Yoga Society, *Agni Yoga*, para. 23.

This aeroperil would not have an effect upon our mechanism if it were not contaminated with imperil. The only way to escape the danger of aeroperil is to purify our nerve channels from imperil.

> *... When irritation has an impersonal cosmic character, its poison may be removed by a current of prana. But if conceit or self-pity intensify the irritation, then the sediment of poison will be precipitated upon the centers. Then there is no means to eject it; one may only wear it away by cosmic perception.*
>
> *Quality of thinking must be realized as a curative. The quality of gratitude is likewise the finest purification of the organism.... Great is the healing power of the emission of gratitude....*
> Agni Yoga Society, *Agni Yoga*, para. 31.

Imperil not only brings disaster to our organism, but it

> *... permeates the space, for the purity of which we all are responsible.*
> Agni Yoga Society, *Agni Yoga*, para. 221.

People of continuous irritation must be avoided. They

contaminate not only space, but can contaminate the place where you live, the place where you sleep, or the place where you work. This is the reason why contact with certain people leaves us in an exhausted and confused state of being. Imperil can enter into your etheric body and aura, and weaken your vitality; many colds are the result of weakening your vitality through imperil.

In olden times, people used to have sanctuaries in their homes where they communicated with the Highest. No one was permitted to enter there. Such a sanctuary or a room in your home can be a refuge for you to go and tune yourself with Higher Forces and vitalize all your being.

Sometimes imperil is transmitted by the so-called "evil eye" into fruits, water, and objects. Fruits become tasteless, water becomes bitter, and objects break. It is possible to taste imperil from the fruit partially eaten by someone who is full of imperil. The same thing can be done by drinking water left in a glass from which another one drank. Imperil is also transmitted through touch. Articles used or touched by a person in irritation or full of imperil will even transmit imperil to other articles, which, in turn, will pass the imperil on to those who use the article.

The same is true of food. It makes a difference who cooks the food and who serves the food. Food can be contaminated by imperil if the person is full of irritation. This is why wealthy families used to hire only those servants and cooks who were naturally joyful, content, and happy.

Imperil is transmitted most directly through intercourse or kissing on the mouth. Desire-energy channels imperil into the other party, thus sharing their imperil. A handshake does the same thing. Shoes, socks, towels, and shirts can be easily contaminated by imperil. One must try to use his own objects and discard them periodically, even if they are not worn out. Pencils, pens, and books carry heavy imperil if they were used by an irritated person. Our libraries are full of imperil.

It is interesting that water does not transmit imperil, although it absorbs it. Thoughts and emotions charged by imperil travel by land, but not by water, except through objects. Lakes, seas, oceans, and rivers break collective transmissions of imperil. Islands are very appropriate for advanced spiritual work in the higher realms and for deeper creative work.

Bliss can be transmitted by water. If a holy man swims in a pool, that pool is charged with bliss, and whoever enters in shares the bliss. But imperil is imprisoned in water and cannot be transmitted through your skin. It can be transmitted to one who drinks such water, and then he becomes contaminated by it.

Baptismal water and bliss energy wash away accumulated imperil from the physical and astral plane. The shock of enlightenment cleanses imperil from the mental plane.

Contemporary man gets into frequent troubles by having close contacts with many people emanating imperil throughout their systems. Pretty faces, pretty clothes, high rank and titles are no guarantee that one does not have imperil. Heavy layers of imperil are found in public officials because they are continuously under the attacks of irritation. Courtrooms and prisons emanate heavy strata of imperil.

People in certain countries in the East do not like to buy houses which were occupied previously by people who had tensions, fights, disputes or continuous irritation. They go and meet the people who previously occupied the house. If they are creative, harmonious people, people dedicated to the Common Good and high ideals, they prefer to buy their houses, even if they are structurally not too satisfactory. In the West, no one asks who lived in a house if the house meets his physical needs.

In a certain place there was a house in which a holy man used to live. Many people were anxious to buy that house "because," they thought, "the emanations of the holy man will be the transmitter of blessings."

We notice sometimes that our psychological and health problems began to appear the day we moved to another house, or bought an old piece of furniture, a carpet, or a painting which was used by another person. Investigation will show that these objects were carrying imperil from their former owners, and that we contaminated our place by bringing them in. This would have been considered a superstition fifty years ago, but we now know that psychic emanations stick to objects and influence people in close contact with them.

I remember one day my uncle brought a sofa to our house. One of his friends was leaving the country and had given it to him. He brought it to our house, feeling that my mother would be happy to use it. A few days later in conversation my uncle mentioned to whom the sofa used to belong. My mother's face changed, and she went to the kitchen and pretended she was cooking something until my uncle left. Immediately after my uncle left, she called me to help her. To my surprise she told me to open the big window on the second floor. We lifted the sofa and threw it from the window to the garden where it broke into pieces. "Mother," I exclaimed, "it was a good-looking sofa." "Yes," she answered, "but good appearance does not mean that it has not been polluted by the emanations of a man who threw his wife and children out and spent his life gambling, drinking, and cursing in his house. We do not need that influence in our home." The next day, my father burned it in the fireplace.

Thoughts are forces. Feelings are forces. Imperil in space is a contagious force which penetrates into objects. On the other hand, highly charged spiritual thoughts can purify space. Our speeches or words carry either light and bliss, or poison and darkness. Places where criminal thoughts and words were or are being used continuously can contaminate our aura, weaken us, and prevent us from contacting higher forces. . . . *The senseless words rise like black whirlwinds. It is dangerous to defile the space.* . . .

Agni Yoga Society, *Agni Yoga*, para. 367.

We are told that the Teaching must be given without irritation. Personal glamors and illusions, or character defects must be discussed without personal implication, expectation or imposition of ideas.

It is sometimes better if one refrains from quarrels, fights, and relationships which cause irritation. We are told that often Holy Ones keep silent and indifferent on occasions where the possibility of irritation and imperil exists. It is also good to know that . . . *One does not have to be a giant of thought in order to harm. Even a mediocre thought poisoned by the crystal of imperil will be very effective.* . . .

Agni Yoga Society, *Hierarchy*, para. 125.

Thoughts carry imperil, which is one of the reasons why some great Initiates and disciples like to work behind the scenes so as not to attract negative thoughts of people polluted with imperil. Thus they can create better, being free from the pressure and pollution of thoughts full of the crystals of imperil. This also applies to ourselves. Every time we are irritated and direct our negative thoughts to others, we literally send them poison or imperil through our thoughts. Thus one should be careful about his thoughts, especially when his body is full of imperil.

Positively charged thoughts, thoughts which carry great ideas, visions, and revelations can eliminate part or all of the poison from our system. This is why meditation is, in itself, a healing process which also charges space with beauty.

We are advised to stay away from those people whose mental body is polluted with imperil. Often it is better to escape than to fight with our thoughts. Irritation and imperil activate germs. Germs are more active and contagious when the holder of the germs is in irritation. One is not susceptible to germs until his aura is weakened by irritation and imperil.

It is better not to eat or communicate with people when the flames of irritation are already consuming our aura. Eating will increase imperil. One must not go to sleep in this condition. He must calm himself with prayer first. A long time ago, Christ warned us, "Let not the sun set upon your anger." Anger is a violent form of irritation. In the Teaching we are told that . . . *the Chinese sometimes fed the enemy with the liver of an irritated rooster. . . .*

Agni Yoga Society, *Heart*, para. 534.

The ancients warned us not to eat when angry or irritated because the food we eat will turn into poison through irritation and imperil and cause greater trouble in our system.

We are always advised to pray before we eat or keep silence for a few minutes and invoke the joy and blessings of the heavenly world. Such an act will prevent the possibility of irritation, and the food will carry the needed energy to the system.

We see that bad news is often given to us at the dinner table, or heavy, angry discourse is carried on while eating. Such habits will soon cost heavily, not only through our health, but through the savings account, too. I was living in a home with a family for three months. They had three children, and their father used to work for the railway station. At five o'clock he used to come home, take a shower, and sit at the table to eat. After the dishes were served and they started to eat, the mother used to tell him what his children did during the day.

"Your oldest boy broke the windows of the neighbor's house."

"Yeah?"

"Your daughter broke the violin."

"Yeah?"

This continued until one day I noticed that the poor man never finished his food, but making some excuse, departed from the table. For several days he did not come to eat and excused himself by saying that he had eaten with his friends. One day I asked him why he was not eating with the family any more. He replied, "I cannot digest when I eat at my home. My wife poisons my mood." The man died of a strange sickness at the age of forty-five.

> . . . *Imperil must not only be recognized as the calamity of the departing race, but the contagion of the imperil should also be studied. It will be possible to ascertain that imperil acts upon far distances and can affect the subtle body.* . . .
> Agni Yoga Society, *Hierarchy*, para. 335.

One occasionally feels the effect of thoughts charged with imperil. Sensitive people are attacked by such thoughts. That is why the Teaching advises us to guard our thoughts because they travel and can spread poison in space and contaminate people.

It is also very interesting to know that

> *... People who depart from Earth with a store of imperil create for themselves a torturous existence; the fire of space rushes upon them. ... Each opposition to the foundations calls forth the counteraction of the fire of space. Thus, one should admit that personal irritation is the defect of the departing ones. ...*
> Agni Yoga Society, **Hierarchy**, para. 335.

Astral forces and dark ones from the mental plane can penetrate people's aura and even poison them if their astral and mental bodies are contaminated with imperil. Many mediums, automatic writers, and lower psychics are the dwelling places of such dark entities. Such people often demonstrate heavy irritation, which proves that their messages are coming from doubtful sources.

> *... after obsession the gates remain open to visitors for a long time. Very intense observation is needed to protect the one who has admitted an obsessor through irritation, which opens wide the door. The heart is the best protection against obsession, but one must watch that the heart should not fall asleep.*
> Agni Yoga Society, **Heart**, para. 169.

> *... only greatness of heart will preserve one from the poison of irritation ....*
> Agni Yoga Society, **Heart**, para. 277.

> *... irritation full of imperil opens the entrance*

> *for the dark ones. Where there is irritation various newcomers set themselves to profit by it and increase the action of the poison. . . .*
> Agni Yoga Society, *Heart*, para. 93.

As irritation continues, imperil increases day after day, gradually tearing away etheric webs and penetrating into higher bodies. It is through such cracks that the dark ones settle themselves within the aura of a human being and help to increase the destructive effect of the poison.

> *Chiefly, learn to think in solitude. And realize responsibility of thought. Verily, thought levels the strongest walls. Doubt, irritation, and self-pity can be consciously ejected. I advise to observe oneself and remember that no one else besides the Teacher will help. I advise to regard the Teacher as the only stronghold.*
> Agni Yoga Society, *Agni Yoga*, para. 340.

"The Teacher" can be our Higher Self or our Master Who has conquered time, space, and matter, and Who will help us overcome doubt, irritation, and self-pity. It is beautiful to note that "only the Teacher will help," because it is only the Teacher who is interested in your highest good. The strongest bond exists between the Teacher and the disciple.

The solitude referred to here is an insulated state of consciousness. Such a consciousness can absorb the thoughts of the Higher Self and fill the mind with light and beauty. In a non-isolated state, the thoughtwaves of others reach us and distort our thoughts, or even replace our thoughts.

Doubt, irritation, and self-pity can be consciously ejected. Of course this requires a disciplined mind which is under the control of the Self and is able to eject these attacks of doubt, irritation, and self-pity. Doubt is mental confusion in which your mind, being identified with an event or phenomenon, loses faith in the Essence, in the Self, either in you or in the universe.

Irritation is a state in which you let your nervous system respond to incoming unpleasant or destructive influences, energies or impressions. Self-pity is a state in which you are identified with your little self. It is a state of Self-denial. For the time being you forget about the Real Self. In that state you feel that you are left out and no one is really interested in you. All these three enemies of the Self can be ejected consciously by not letting them gain control upon you.

In the New Testament you can see a great example of the ability to eject irritation, doubt, and self-pity when, in intense suffering on the cross, Christ said, "Forgive them, Father, for they do not know what they are doing." What a magnificent way to reject doubt, irritation, and self-pity. We have a similar example in the story of Socrates, who drank the poison with utmost serenity. They both knew that the last hour of their lives should not be contaminated by imperil.

Irritation is the automatic resistance of our nervous system, or etheric, astral, and mental bodies to incoming impressions, either positive or negative. Our nervous system and our subtle bodies have a natural resistance to all those negative impressions which are harmful to them. When such harmful impressions hit these mechanisms, they emanate a vaporous element which creates a sphere of protection around them. It is similar to what the white blood cells do to intruders.

When the harmful impressions continue to bombard beyond the limits of the energy resources of these mechanisms, they yield and feel tired, and the vaporous emanations burn and turn into nerve-ashes, into sediments. This is what imperil is.

There are three kinds of resistance:
1. automatic resistance
2. conscious negative resistance
3. conscious positive resistance or discriminative rejection

Automatic resistance is a natural, protective mechanism. For example, you have physiological changes in your eyes and ears when you have the impressions of excess light or sound. The nervous system and the subtle bodies react similarly to incoming negative impressions.

Conscious negative resistance starts when you register the incoming impressions and hate them, curse them, become angry with them, but do not take a positive action to eliminate their causes.

Conscious positive resistance or discriminative rejection occurs when you register the incoming impressions and take physical and physiological steps to shut them off, divert them, or use them in creative ways if possible. For example, you are traveling by railway and you continuously feel irritated by the clickety-clack of the wheels passing through the railway joints. Now if you are a musical talent, you can use this situation as a rhythm and compose some music, as Beethoven did while riding in a carriage — without being irritated.

Another example: You have a person who continuously acts in a silly and inconsiderate way, and you feel you have every right to be irritated. In conscious positive resistance you think of how to react to that person so that his behavior becomes a real help to you in developing patience, understanding, and compassion.

Most of the sources of irritation can be handled through conscious positive resistance. This can be learned as an art, if one has the spirit of a sportsman. For example, all dangerous moves of a tennis player can be taken as an impetus for a better return. Or the organizational activities of the dark forces can evoke greater solemnity, wisdom, and daring from you. Thus most of the unfavorable conditions of life, instead of creating irritation, evoke courage, reasoning, stability, balance, daring, and wisdom from you.

We must be able to say in the future that one will be able to annihilate the possibility of poisoning from imperil if one assumes a conscious positive resistance to the challenges of life. We must remember that conscious positive resistance can be exercised only on the plane where our focus of consciousness is.

There are irritation-causing subtle waves which come from solar or galactic sources. Most of us are unprotected from such waves because they are recorded on our higher mental or Intuitional planes, and our consciousness usually functions on the lower mental planes, or even on the physical plane. These kinds of irritation-causing waves usually can be rejected unconsciously if a person's aura is full of the essence of love, joy, and bliss, and the overall tonality of the aura is in harmony with Cosmic directions.

There is also a mysterious source of irritation which can be called the result of indigestion of the Teaching and inability to apply It to life. The roots of such irritation are very deep. Collected wisdom and beauty build a set of standards in the inner being of the person, but as he fails to live these standards in life and apply them to the world, he creates an inner friction, which is sometimes called frustration and the sense of failure. Such an inner state creates irritation and the resultant imperil.

If imperil reaches a certain stage of density, it not only brings great harm to the physical and subtle mechanisms of man, but it also destroys the formations of the standards and makes him feel really poor, miserable, and vacant. This is the reason for some mysterious changes that people sometimes witness in others who suddenly renounce their principles and follow the path of their lower urges and drives.

There is also a condition in which the positive inflow of impressions creates irritation in certain people. The first reason is that those people react through their hang-ups, wounds, posthypnotic suggestions, and through the registration of their painful experiences. No matter how much love and tenderness you express, they will feel irritated. For example, your nose reminds them of one who in the past caused them suffering. Or, because they are loaded with such a great amount of imperil, any positive impression is absorbed by their imperil, making it more active, inflammable, and destructive. Mostly the imperil of such people is found in the channels of their mental and astral networks.

It is very difficult to reach such people with positive impressions because the majority of their centers of reception are blocked by imperil and only a few stand open. One must be very accurate in finding through which door he can reach the imprisoned soul, bypassing fears, posthypnotic suggestions, and the watchdogs of association.

Hypnotism is a wrong effort to reach the "soul" because it pushes away the soul and replaces him by a hypnotic command. In such a case the unconscious friction between the posthypnotic suggestion and the soul becomes a source of irritation and imperil.

People have very peculiar notions about pain and suffering. They think that pain and suffering expand their consciousness and make them more human. But the things that they learn during the time of pain and suffering become posthypnotic suggestions in their minds. Later, they act under these posthypnotic suggestions and raise their children under their influence. Most fanatic parents who force their will on their children or on others act under such hypnosis. For example, suppose you are beating and insulting your child because he is refusing to believe your religion or tradition, and while you are beating him you are saying to him, "You must follow the faith of your forefathers or else there is no salvation for you." This child will take your order as a posthypnotic suggestion and eventually, maybe years later, will learn about your faith, and he will teach others in the same way you taught him, and he will make others follow his faith in the same way you wanted him to follow yours.

Thus pain and suffering will block his questioning mind and he will miss seeing the new conditions, the changing conditions in the world which require new attitudes and free choice. But the greater damage will be registered when, during the time of imparting the tradition to others, he will key in with your image and with his image of the past and repeat the same state of irritation you and he had.

Obsolete superstitions are perpetuated from generation to generation because all are taught through pain and suffering. Thus, as much as possible, one must avoid irritation for himself and for others. Anything of value, when mixed with irritation, becomes a source of trouble and a perpetuating factor of irritation and imperil. One of my Teachers used to say, "Things that are taught in the spirit of joy, beauty, and freedom remain forever and adapt themselves to the conditions of the changing world."

One may ask, "How do we handle the impressions coming from outer sources upon which we as individuals have no control, such as impressions from various crimes, news, television and radio?" The answer will be: through the practice of *detachment, observation,* and *analysis.*

Any negative impression fails to create irritation if it is approached by a person who knows how to exercise detachment, how to observe things in impersonal ways, and how to analyze them to find out their causes and the process of their formation. Thus a conscious attitude toward negative impressions breaks their charge and even totally rejects them.

Detachment helps us not to be involved and identified with the negative impressions. Observation creates a distance between the object and the observer. The observer comes into being only through a process of observation.

Analysis is the power to disintegrate the impression, weaken it through dissection, and find out the cause of its aggregation and the characteristics of the parts forming the aggregation.

Irritation makes a person take wrong actions and make wrong decisions. It creates wrong imagination, resulting in negative emotions and unintelligent action.

Irritation is the prime cause of depression. In depression the nervous system is saturated with imperil. Depressions of various kinds are due to the accumulation of imperil on various planes. There is physical, emotional, as well as mental depression. On each plane, imperil retards the function of the centers and cuts the flow of energy which creates actions in the vehicle in which the centers are found. When the depression is spread on all planes simultaneously, the soul withdraws out of the aura and the man enters into a coma, lasting for days or weeks. It is the withdrawn human soul who disperses the imperil with psychic energy and when enough purification is achieved, he reoccupies his vehicles.

The physical body has its nervous system. There is a corresponding system in the etheric, astral, and mental bodies, and also there is a communication system — analogous to the nervous system — within the physical and subtle bodies. This nervous system, or the system of etheric nadis (etheric nerve channels) and subtle corresponding mechanisms in the astral and mental planes can be the target, individually or as a whole, of imperil. Whenever imperil comes into being, it spreads slowly to corresponding higher or lower mechanisms.

Imperil creates four dangerous conditions:
1. A blockage of life electricity on the network of the mechanism.
2. Malfunctioning of centers and glands found in the mental, astral, etheric, and physical bodies.
3. Overgrowth of cells to acquire energy.
4. Starvation of cells and degeneration of the body.

On the astral plane, imperil creates whirlpools of forces or crackings which concentrate force in certain parts of the astral body; or make the fiery energy of intuition flow into the astral body and damage certain centers; or open the gates for astral entities to occupy the astral body of man. Whirlpools manifest on the physical plane as various kinds of tumors. Cracks create imbalance, spacing, and emotional turbulences, and stimulate the nervous system over its limits, thereby often creating insomnia and nervous breakdowns.

On the mental plane imperil creates many turbulences which can be symbolized by the words:

>insanity
>negativity
>urge for crime
>depression
>suicidal drives
>separatism

The spiritual entity within the human frame cannot radiate its beauty, love, and light when the networks of communication are blocked by imperil. When spiritual guidance is suspended, man loses his direction and wanders after false values. No matter what his discoveries are, they are used to satisfy his blind urges and drives with an insane judgement, unstable emotions, and a deprived body.

The global aura is full of imperil. One wonders if humanity will be able to heal our sick planet and our sick global aura and once again find a direction toward a healthy planetary and global life.

To protect ourselves from irritation and imperil the following are helpful aids:

1. roses
2. freesias
3. wormwood oil or tea
4. barley
5. musk
6. joy
7. love

8. appreciation
9. recognition of divinity in others
10. self-sacrifice
11. self-forgetfulness
12. harmlessness
13. psychic energy
14. conversation about the Teaching
15. intensification of the spiritual aura
16. striving toward Hierarchy
17. radiation of the heart
18. prayer before sleep
19. prayer before any start of activity
20. insulation of the mind
21. absorption in Self
22. heavy labor
23. periodical change of residence
24. contentment
25. happiness
26. good nourishment
27. proper sleep and complete rest when needed
28. economy of energy
29. orderliness
30. patience
31. expansion of consciousness — expansion of one's own horizon
32. humility
33. sleeping under the stars
34. daring
35. solemnity

1. We are told in the Teaching that *roses* prevent imperil. Ancient kings surrounded their palaces with rose gardens. Some religious groups in Asia use rose oil in their confirmation ceremonies. It was also used to anoint warriors

of the spirit. The absence of imperil makes a man highly creative, clear-minded, enthusiastic, and radioactive. It is possible to use real rose oil in small quantities. You may put a few drops of real rose oil in your bath after cleansing your body in the shower, or you can use it as perfume.

2. *Freesias* strengthen the nervous system and enable it to fight against the accumulating poisons of imperil. Freesias can be planted around the house. Those who need strengthening of their nerves, after passing through some crises or dark nights of the soul, find great assistance in bringing freesias into their rooms and sleeping with the fragrance. This will regulate and calm the nerves.

3. *Wormwood oil* dissolves the heavy layers of imperil, especially in the glands. M.M. recommends it very highly for light external application.

4. *Barley* is very good for the lungs; it strengthens and purifies lungs damaged by the poison of imperil. Barley can be used in soup, and so on.

5. *Musk*, if it is genuine (i.e., taken from the deer), is a very strong disinfectant. It purifies the blood and ejects the residue remaining from imperil. We are told it must be used internally in *very* small granules at certain intervals.

6. *Joy* is a great purifier. When the human soul is in the process of liberation, he radiates joy. His radiation repels those thoughts and emotional currents which carry imperil. By trying to keep ourselves joyful, we not only prevent attacks of imperil, but also prevent the possibility of sending thoughts contaminated with imperil to others. Joy is a special kind of Solar Fire which burns away many polluted currents trying to reach us. Also it purifies the dust of imperil trying to settle in the aura.

It is possible also to direct your joy to any part of your body afflicted by imperil. You can even send your joy to those who are sources of irritation to you. In this way, you prevent, to a high degree, the emanations of imperil from those people.

7. *Love* fused with joy creates miracles. If you really love someone, he cannot irritate you. If you do not love someone, even if he does good things for you, you get irritated by him or by his presence. Love builds a shield around you and makes you understand others.

8. Many people are irritated because of lack of *appreciation* for what they do or of what they are. Appreciation releases tensions, prevents irritation, and lets loose the love energy in others and in ourselves. Appreciation allows the person to feel his dignity, his value, and relate on a higher level of consciousness. Appreciation prevents imperil from multiplying or spreading. Appreciation is the ability to see the divinity and its expressions. Wherever divinity or higher values are emphasized, imperil has little chance to succeed.

9. *Recognition of divinity in others.* This is a higher quality than appreciation. In all conditions and circumstances, you see the presence of divinity, the hand of divinity. In all men, even in the most corrupted one, you recognize divinity and try to bring out that divinity through your recognition. Your recognition helps them to adjust their personality expressions to the Inner Divinity.

Very often the Divine Hand touches you in a way you do not like, and you develop high-voltage irritation. But if you recognize the Divine Hand, you appreciate Its blows because you know that it is all for your own highest interests.

10. *Self-sacrifice* is a steady flow of Beauty,

Goodness, and Truth. Every time you have an attack you can counterbalance it with self-sacrifice which can be expressed as sacrificial acts. For example, if someone stole your ring, instead of irritation, think that you can sacrifice it for someone who was eager enough to dare to steal it. Or if someone tries to hurt and irritate you, think you do not exist. It is our pride in the false self that creates resistance and hence, irritation.

11. *Self-forgetfulness* is the ability to remove your self-interest from any transactions with your friends and enemies, and look upon things as they are. For example, if you are arguing about something and you are relating yourself to the subject and the outcome of the argument, you will not be able to see the issues; you will not be able to debate for the sake of facts and reality. As soon as both partners remove their selves from the debate or argument, the facts will emerge clearly. In all our relationships, the self must be forgotten if we do not want irritation to settle within ourselves.

12. *Harmlessness* is the ability to relate to people in such a way that their progress on the path is not hindered by your acts, words, emotions, thoughts, and plans. When you irritate people or become irritated by people, you are hurting not only others but also yourself. Harmlessness is the ability not to be affected by the irritations of others and not to irritate others. A harmless man creates a shicld in his aura which repels arrows of imperil.

One day my Teacher told me to hurry and open the big window in the hall and come back to see him immediately. I rushed and opened the window and hurried to him sitting behind a tree. He pointed out an angry boy who was walking very carefully, looking around himself. Then we saw him stop in front of the hall, throw a big rock through the open window, and quickly run away, disappearing behind the bushes. When the rock flew into the hall, the Teacher very calmly said, "Often open your doors and windows when attacked." This is an example of indifference and harmlessness. Later the boy was walking in the garden, acting as if he had not thrown the rock through the open window. The Teacher approached him and said, "Rocks thrown at open windows will fall into your being, and it will be very difficult to find them and clean them out." He was referring to imperil.

13. *Psychic energy*, if invoked or applied, not only melts away the imperil, but also causes all poisonous darts of the dark ones to bounce back. Psychic energy galvanizes the nervous system and increases the purifying fires in the centers and in the glands. Psychic energy is prana for the nerves.

14. *Conversation about the Teaching*. The Teacher advises us not to surrender ourselves to idle thoughts, gossip, criticism, or use our tongues for commonplace curses and hateful expressions. All these are sources of irritation. By conversing about the Teaching, we raise the vibration in the room and draw psychic energy and beneficent devas who love the colors of higher ideas, visions, and thoughts. Such conversation channels the energy of Great Ones. In such an atmosphere irritation and imperil cannot dwell, as snow cannot exist in a hot place.

15. *Intensification of the spiritual aura*. Such an aura is built or created by our spiritual living, by expressing the virtues of the Soul, of divine ideas and beauty in our daily life. Our aura is the pool of all emanations of our vehicles and the Self. If it is radiant with pure lights and colors, it will be a great shield preventing imperil from

penetrating our bodies, or dissolving imperil produced within our system. This is why Great Ones want us to live the Teaching and create a new frequency in our lives, expressing the highest within us through all our actions, feelings and thoughts.

16. *Striving toward the Hierarchy.* Striving produces psychic energy. It orients the whole mechanism toward the Soul. It draws the energy of Hierarchy. The energy of the Hierarchy is joy, bliss, and peace. Every time a man strives toward the Hierarchy, he releases a new electrical charge from his Core, from his Self, which renews the old tissues and gives them vitality and drive to exert themselves. Exertion clears away imperil and does not allow irritation to be deposited in the nervous system. The energy of the Hierarchy is the greatest protection when its circulatory flow is not impeded in your system.

17. *Radiation of the heart.* This radiation is compassion. Also, it is the light of life, the light of the One Life. The heart is a fountain of the life of the Cosmic Existence. When our heart center is open, when the heart center in the head is awake, then we transmit the life electricity of that Great Existence. It burns and purifies all that does not agree with the heartbeat of the Cosmic Heart. We must learn to practically radiate this compassion, this life electricity, in all our relationships. It is this radiation which will repel all possibility of irritation and imperil.

18. *Prayer before sleep.* Prayer before sleep is recommended by the Great Ones. It lifts the heart to a higher dimension, so that when man sleeps he does not fall into the lower strata of the etheric, astral or mental planes, but contacts the targets of his prayers as far as possible, avoiding the danger of lower frequencies. Such a sleep

invigorates the etheric and physical bodies, which then fight better against imperil. Sometimes when prayer is really deep and tunes in with great centers, spiritual beings accompany you while your body is in sleep, protecting not only you, but also your physical body.

19. *Prayer before any start of activity.* Hindus repeat OM whenever they want to start new work. Muslims have their mantram which says, "There is no One else except God." Some Christians say, "In the name of Christ," and others use different expressions, but the essence is the same. The purpose of such behavior is to shield you by the invoked power of the Almighty One to meet any situation, any condition and reaction with the indifference of spiritual power. When such a spirit increases in you, you can face almost any situation in life without being shocked or confused. Your prayers link you, not only with the Highest within you, but also with the Highest in the universe. Prayers protect you from involvement in irritation and imperil.

20. *Insulation of the mind.* This is a technique that great disciples use to withdraw their attention from anything that is low, negative, hostile or destructive. In this insulation they are aware of all that is going on in the lower planes, but they are not involved in it. This can be cultivated through concentration exercises.

21. *Absorption in Self.* This is a more advanced stage when your awareness is absorbed in the Spiritual Triad, or even in the Self, and you observe the outer things without the slightest irritation. Sometimes such a state is called ecstasy, nirvana or bliss, in which no hostile arrow reaches you, and you radiate serenity and bliss in spite of the storms taking place in the lower strata. This state can be reached through meditation and contemplation.

22. *Heavy labor* is a means to crack and melt away imperil, and to strengthen the network of your nervous system. Heavy labor eventually releases those beneficent secretions of your glands which clear the imperil and repair its damage in tissues and organs. Heavy labor also draws energy from the secret chambers of the centers which, like hidden reservoirs, contain energies only released under higher pressure. These energies have a great purificatory effect on your system.

23. *Periodical change of residence.* Sometimes it is very wise to leave a place where quarrels, irritations, and negative states of mind, emotions, and body were in existence. It is very interesting to note that in proportion to an increased altitude, imperil decreases. High mountains and pure air carry more prana and psychic energy, which are beneficent vitamins to rehabilitate the health of those hurt by irritation and imperil. High deserts and, curiously enough, the air and water of the ocean have the same curative quality.

One not only must move from his dwelling place, but also sometimes from the city, from the state, and from the country, if necessary. Moving away, if consciously done, helps to eliminate many future dangers to physical and mental health, and to increase creativity. But one must not have the illusion that only changing places itself is beneficial. New places must be chosen with great discrimination.

24. *Contentment.* This is not satisfaction with what you are or have. Contentment is a spiritual serenity in which the conditions of your personality and its environment cannot disturb your peace and spirit contact. You are happy and content in the bliss of your spirit, in spite of adverse conditions in the lower world. Contentment gives you a very detached way to work to change the conditions

of life without being contaminated by them.

25. *Happiness.* A happy person repels irritation. Irritation cannot build its nest in a happy man. That is why one must not only be joyful, but also happy. People have difficulty discriminating between these two. Joy is the state of the human soul who is not identified with the personality. Happiness is a state of the soul who is identified with the personality and enjoys the life in the personality. Happy people and happy surroundings help one to not fall into the trap of irritation.

> *Not discontent, nor irritation, but the sensation of happiness is necessary; because it is verily happiness to create the works of the Teacher.*
>
> Agni Yoga Society, *Agni Yoga*, para. 368.

True happiness is the result of health, positive emotions, clear thinking, and a giving heart.

26. *Good food and good nourishment* are essential for the body, because a weak body is a hotbed for germs and feeds imperil. The sediments of imperil are nourished in the decay of our body, emotions, and mind. Decaying emotional and mental substances serve as food for imperil.

A strong and healthy body will also help the health of the astral and mental body, for it does not give a chance for imperil to spread and multiply, or cause additional irritation. A man on the path will take care of his body through right diet, right exercise, and sufficient sleep. Undernourished people produce imperil. One of the services of the disciples is to teach humanity the right diet and help to distribute food to those who are suffering from malnutrition.

27. *Proper sleep and complete rest when needed.* Proper sleep falls between the period of 10:00 p.m. and

5:00 a.m. In higher altitudes one may reduce the hours of sleep. Sleep not only repairs the damaged parts of the body, but strengthens the nerves to fight irritation and the resultant imperil. A child who has not slept enough is irritable. A nursing mother who did not rest enough is irritable and feeds her child imperil through her milk. That is why in olden times the woman was forbidden to breast-feed the child when she was irritated or in habitual irritation.

Rest is the absence of conflict within your mind, within your emotional and physical bodies. It is a state of contentment and joy. It is a state of harmony and equilibrium. You can even be in rest at the time of your highest striving toward achievement. Rest is a state of withdrawal from conflicting and inharmonious situations and entering into a state where there is balance, solution, understanding and striving toward Infinity. Rest is the ability to be honest with oneself and with others. Rest is purity of heart. Rest is harmlessness. Rest is merging with the unchanging reality within your Core.

When the Great Ones suggest for us to rest, They do not want us to go and lie down and sink into inertia. They suggest for us to harmonize all our actions and expressions with the rhythm of our Spiritual Core. True rest is the absence of contradictory activities, emotions, and thoughts, when you enter into the sphere of beauty, harmony, love, truth and goodness within you and relax all conflicting centers within your system. The tension of striving opens the gates of rest, and dissipates imperil. Irritation is the absence of rest. Imperil does not come into existence when one is in harmony within himself and the universe. Harmony is rest.

28. *Economy of energy.* Most imperil multiplies and crystallizes on the nerve channels because of lack of

energy wasted by excessive sexual activity on physical, emotional, and mental levels. Sexual reactions and habits are a great source of irritation to people. Often people try to get rid of irritation and frustration by exhausting their energies, but they fall into a greater trap because as they waste them, they become more prone to irritation.

The way to overcome irritation resulting from sexual license is through economy and self-control, in directing your attention to higher visions and plans of service. M.M. once suggested that one even must not do any unnecessary movement because it wastes energy. The economy of energy is imperative for those who are preparing to climb higher summits of achievement.

29. *Orderliness.* Orderliness is a great prevention of irritation. Many people are irritated when they lose something, when they misplace something, or when there is no order and harmony in their surroundings. A secretary who does not know where a certain letter is will be irritated by searching for it. A man of order will be irritated to see a desk or an office where a chaotic condition exists. Such conditions weigh heavily on our nervous system and cause irritation.

It can also be noticed that usually disorderly people are those who are easily caught in irritation and have a great amount of imperil. Imperil makes people lethargic and leads them to apathy.

30. *Patience.* Patience is a great shield against irritation. When one learns how to be patient, he cuts ninety percent of the sources of irritation. Patience is an ability to draw oneself into the domain of the future and Infinity.

. . . It is a solace to know that patience over-

comes any irritation. In the intensity of patience a special substance is created which, like a powerful antidote, neutralizes even imperil. But, of course, patience is not a lack of feeling. During criminal indifference, benevolent reactions are not evident. Patience is a conscious tension and an opposition to darkness.

Agni Yoga Society, **Heart**, para. 478.

In the esoteric teaching great emphasis was placed on patience, and special conditions were created to cultivate patience. In one of the schools in the East the following training schedule for patience was used:

a. Walk two miles daily with joy, love, and a smile.
b. First walk two miles daily; then three miles; then five miles. Continue this for six months without any complaint or vexation.
c. Joyfully refrain from eating at the dinner table while others eat.
d. Postpone pleasures of any kind.
e. Try to be silent and indifferent in trying conditions.
f. Exercise inner and outer reticence.
g. Postpone your reactions in certain exciting occasions to people and objects, and keep your serenity.
h. Lock yourself in your home for a few days and avoid feeling lonely or depressed.
i. Take a laborious job and finish it with full attention. For example, mix fifteen thousand beads of colors and string them on a thread in a special numerical sequence: one red, three yellow, two green, five orange, and so on. Make sure there is

a harmonious pattern. When you are finished, undo it, and start again.

j. Baby-sit a hyperactive child after deciding that no matter what he does, you will act totally indifferent.

k. Exercise patience in your reactions to all your family and friends.

l. Try to be calm and joyful whenever people are late in their personal appointments or in keeping their promises.

As a whole, teach your personality patience. Patience develops in you as you expand your sense of Infinity.

Irritation is closely connected with impatience. Impatience accelerates the damage of imperil in our system. Curiously enough, impatience directs imperil from the solar plexus area into the sex organs and extremities of the body.

31. *Expansion of consciousness* lets greater rays penetrate into our system and enables us not to be affected by the ripples of the ocean of life. By expanding our consciousness, we prevent the attacks of irritation caused by separative viewpoints and separative interests. Irritation has a very close kinship with the spirit of separation. Expansion of consciousness bridges many gaps of separatism and thus blocks the source of irritation.

One is in irritation because another religion exists, another interpretation of the same religion exists, or another nation or another interest exists. Expansion of consciousness cleans such sources of irritation and leads the man into unity. It is seldom that irritation exists in one who has a unified field of consciousness.

One day history will reveal that human suffering came through those people who, because of their separative attitude, developed irritation and imperil and produced plans for destruction.

32. *Humility* is the spiritual ability by which you can stay unhurt in spite of attacks coming to you in many forms through various sources. Humility does not resist evil, although it annihilates the root of it, the cause of it. People think that humility is a sign of weakness. It is not so. True humility is the result of possession of a great power and wisdom which does not counterattack. Instead, humility holds the hand of the aggressor until the hand feels numb, but then he smiles and lets it go to digest the lesson.

Humility is being a great mountain which is not moved by winds or attacks. A man is humble because he knows it is the Great Self that is the source of all wisdom and power. Through humility irritation is rejected.

33. *Sleeping under the stars* when there is no moonlight, or when one is shielded from the moonlight is very beneficial for the nervous system. It greatly helps to minimize irritation. The rays of the stars and galaxies are the radiation of great Spirits, great Entities. It is possible to accumulate them in our higher planes through meditation or contemplation, and dispel the imperil out of our system. One can reach the same result by concentrating all his being on future visions.

34. *Daring.* Psychic energy can be increased through acts of daring. When one lets loose the concentrated focus of energy within one's Innermost Being to achieve new heights of creativity and sacrificial service, the psychic energy pours into one's aura, with blue and red flames. It is this energy which builds a shield around us and burns all

attacks of irritation, imperil, and fear.

A great Sage says,

> *... In time of confusion, of course, psychic energy cannot be condensed so as to begin to act. But through daring of the spirit psychic energy can burst forth as a powerful flame, forming, as it were, a shield against encroaching evil....*
>
> Agni Yoga Society, *Fiery World, Vol. III*, para. 413.

35. *Solemnity* is the ability to dwell and remain in the presence of the Inner Guide, and in the presence of the Master. Such an attitude enables you to look upon life from the viewpoint and measures of the Soul and Master. Solemnity is the ability to stand within your essential Self and have a detached outlook on the trivial interests of life.

> *... one must preserve solemnity, because this feeling will not allow small and futile irritations and decay.*
>
> Agni Yoga Society, *Heart*, para. 435.

> *... It is not without reason that I reiterate about solemnity, because it is the nourishment of the heart! Not by condemnation or irritation, but in solemnity do we prepare for the great march onward.*
>
> Agni Yoga Society, *Heart*, para. 462.

Through solemnity we radiate our spiritual achievements, and inspire and encourage people to strive. Condemnation and irritation bind people to past images and prevent them from looking toward the future.

Solemnity feeds the heart. It is in the heart that the spirit is anchored. The spirit shines like a pure flame as solemnity feeds its. In reality, the spirit is a heart-shaped flame. The reflection is what we call "the heart." Solemnity is the moment of the sunrise within us.

> . . . one should be able to pass at least one day without the slightest irritation. Imperil corrodes the most significant reflexes of energy. . . . The most significant results are obscured by one crystal of imperil. Imperil should not be regarded as a houseplant, its odor is wide-spreading and blights all currents. Hence, when I speak against irritation, I do not refer to dogma, but to an indicated medical cure. As always, this consideration must be carried out beginning with the most minute. . . .
>
> Agni Yoga Society, *Heart*, para. 465.

Psychic energy radiates out of our bodies. It can even be impressed on film if irritation and imperil do not interfere. Most of the efforts to photograph subtle emanations fail because the photographer and the one to be photographed cannot stay one day without irritation. M.M. says, *Imperil corrodes the most significant reflexes of the energy.* Thus many psychic experiments fail because of irritation and imperil.

It is true also that some very learned and able people cannot impress others and lead them toward the path of unfoldment and beauty. Irritation and imperil existing in their nature prevent these currents from reaching them, or it pollutes the currents in such a way that they create reverse results: rejection, indifference, even betrayal. It is possible to have great visions, great inspirations, but live a barren life — because of the imperil existing within your body.

Creativity increases as the occasions of irritation decrease. The absence of irritation is the moment of creativity. Creativity is manifestation of inner Beauty, Goodness, and Truth. Many promising artists fail on their path of success when they tolerate irritation moving in and poisoning all their being.

There exists also the imitation of art, such as disco music, acid and rock music, which transmits heavy dosages of imperil. The victims of such music feel a strong urge to use drugs and smoke marijuana to tranquilize their irritation. This usage is even worse than the music, because combined with irritation, drugs and marijuana produce more imperil.

Certain movies are transmitters of irritation and imperil. This is why M.M., referring to irritation says, . . . *It is imperative to expel this beast from the house.* . . .
Agni Yoga Society, *Community*, para. 78.

Imperil not only prevents radioactivity of the Inner Self through real creative work and livingness, but also prevents or distorts the energy flow of "White Forces." When humanity is overcast by a layer of imperil, the forces of the Hierarchy and the forces of the Stronghold cannot create the conditions for conscious response from humanity. This is how many races were degenerated on the path of human history.

Great Beings and Existences expressing Themselves through great suns and constellations can impress us and expect conscious registration of Their messages only when our receptive apparatus is clean from the sediments of imperil. In many brotherhoods there is a special rule that irritation must be kept away from group gatherings or meetings. The leader advises all members and suggests not attending if they have any grudge in their hearts against another member. They thought that if such persons were present in the group or meetings, they would continuously produce imperil and pollute the group, the meeting, and the membership in general.

More advanced members are instructed to stay away from any committee or from any serious affairs of the group and isolate themselves for a while until the attack of irritation is exhausted. The same instruction was given to the families of the leaders. They should practically isolate the irritated members of their families in guest rooms until by right approach and proper treatment the attack is overcome.

In the Teaching we read, . . . *When pepper dust is in the air, all begin to sneeze. Thus can imperil be spread.* . . .
Agni Yoga Society, *Fiery World, Vol. I*, para. 161.

In advanced meetings where decisive actions would be taken, the leadership used to keep the meetings as far as possible on Soul or transpersonal levels, and if in rare cases irritation crept in, they used to adjourn the meeting until further notice. They used to think that any decision taken in irritation may lead to destructive results or to failure. In an irritated atmosphere many dark forces exercise their influences. That is why we are told that decisions must be taken in silence and in serenity.

The Teaching says that . . . *Nothing so irritates the fiery element as disorderly thinking.* . . .
Agni Yoga Society, *Fiery World, Vol. I*, para. 247.

A man can fall into disorderly thinking for various reasons:
   a. Lack of personality integration.
   b. A disintegration process going on in his personality because of imperil, fear, hatred, or doubt.
   c. Damage done to his brain through evil and negative thoughts.

d. Confusion due to a weak foundation.
   e. Standing against the Plan and the Hierarchy.
   f. Knowing the facts and living contrary to his knowledge and beliefs.
   g. The grasp of the agitated emotional body.
   h. Drugs, wrong methods of meditation, smoking, and waste of sexual energy.
   i. Certain psychological exercises, premature discoveries of past lives, and so on.
   j. Release of too much inner light without being ready for it.

Disorderly thinking is like music played on an untuned instrument. When the head centers are not coordinated and in tune with the unfolding twelve-petaled Lotus, thinking has no order. It has no seed, no growth, and no purpose. Such a thought irritates the fiery element in space and in the etheric sphere of man, and evokes violent reactions.

It is very important not to lead people into premature thinking. For example, meditation done by young people will have disastrous effects in their lives if they are less than fifteen years old. It is suggested that they must develop a strong physical, emotional, moral, and aspirational foundation before they engage in serious techniques of thinking.

Many people, even between the ages of twenty and thirty, are not ready for meditation if their physical and emotional development is not expressed through right living. Premature pressure on the brain or mind will result in disorderly thinking which eventually will cause irritation and imperil. The Teaching must never be forced. On the contrary, those who are ready will come and take "the Kingdom of God by violence."

In the Teaching, tension is differentiated from irritation. There is a very subtle difference between them. Tension is the accumulation of energy to perform a labor or to achieve a higher frequency. Irritation is the process of disconnecting the aligned and integrated system. Tension is a gearing process. Irritation is the failure of the gear and the creation of friction. One can achieve through tension, but fail through irritation.

Self-exertion is the result of increasing spiritual tension, but irritation is an act of self-defeat. An irritated person begins to lose control over his mechanism. He loses control of his judgment and sees things in their distorted images.

Irritation short-circuits the electricity of the heart and prevents the current from reaching certain parts of the body. Irritation hinders the warmth of the heart from spreading out.

One of the means of protection from irritation is to repeat the name of Christ. It is also very useful to learn many verses from *The Bhagavad Gita* or from the *Agni Yoga Society* series of books and repeat them on the right occasions. For example, when a beloved one has passed away, you can calm yourself by repeating the following verse from *The Bhagavad Gita*:

> *Verily, there was never a time when I was not, nor you, nor these rulers of men; nor shall come a time when we shall all cease to be.*
> **The Bhagavad Gita**, translated by H. (Torkom) Saraydarian, Chapter 2, Verse 12.

Distant healing is possible if the patient is not irritated.

> *. . . The nerve centers, like fiery vessels, will readily accept the transmission of Agni. . . .*
> Agni Yoga Society, **Fiery World, Vol. I**, para. 518.

If the patient is in irritation, his nerve centers will reject the current of the healing energy. Irritation blocks the nerve channels with imperil.

It is observed that irritation hurts the sight and blocks the current of energy which flows through the eyes and creates contacts. Imperil takes away liveliness from the eyes.

> *Why should evil sometimes seem to be the victor? Only because of the instability of good. By a purely physiological method it can be proved that domination by evil is short-lived. Evil emerges together with imperil, but can at first produce only a strong flash; afterwards it begins to deteriorate and gradually destroys its own progenitor. This means that if Agni is even partially manifested, it will not cease to increase. Thus, when imperil begins to decompose, Agni, on the contrary, acquires its full strength. Therefore I advise that the first attack of evil be endured, in order to leave evil to its own destruction. Moreover, during the duel between evil and good — in other words between imperil and Agni — the latter will grow proportionately, as imperil putrefies its possessor. Thus should one observe the duel between the low and the high, but only a mature consciousness can encourage one to withstand evil. It is useful to remember this and to gather not only strength but also patience, in order to conquer that which is in itself doomed to annihilation. I affirm that the truth, "Light conquers darkness," has even a physiological basis.*
> Agni Yoga Society, *Fiery World, Vol. I*, para. 543.

Imperil is self-destructive and those who produce this poison eventually will be defeated by the poison. The most important thing to do at the time of any attack is to withstand the evil and neutralize oneself by solemnity, magnanimity, and by other means. Immediately, when one finds his equilibrium and invokes the psychic energy or Agni, his position will strengthen over the person carrying imperil. Only through admittance of the entry of imperil and resisting evil, is evil kept alive. This is one of the lessons never learned by humanity as a whole. The defeat of imperil is the increase of the fire of the spirit.

Imperil is like acid which burns its container. One should protect himself and have patience to see the burning of the container. Many groups and many nations who produced imperil vanished forever. Those who are following their steps will have the same destination. But Agni will increase, and the owners of Agni will flourish.

> . . . *People knew long ago that rhythm kindled collective fires and helped in avoiding irritation and disunity.* . . .
> Agni Yoga Society, ***Fiery World, Vol. II***, para. 17.

Rhythmic movements, rhythmic dance, and singing or music were taught in all mystery schools. Rhythm is a great agent of integration. It also releases the fires of the centers in various bodies and regulates their interrelationship.

Physical rhythm is different from emotional rhythm. Emotional rhythm is different from mental, intuitional, atmic, monadic, and divine rhythms. Rhythmic motion expresses the energy corresponding to the plane to which the rhythm is related. Thus certain rhythmic movements transmit etheric, astral or mental energy; they can also transmit higher energies. It is also possible that through certain rhythms a group can transmit zodiacal energies. A different rhythm transmits the energy for each sign.

Rhythmic chanting has similar effects. The energy transmitted spreads not only on the physical, but also on the astral and mental planes, whereas in rhythmic movement, energy is mostly spread in etheric and physical planes.

Rhythmic dancing and singing is the best way to transmit energy to the physical-etheric, astral and mental planes. It is this transmitted psychic energy which purifies the nervous system, glands, and centers and protects man from irritation and imperil. When man is rhythmic, he glows with various fires. Rhythm increases the element of sattva in the personality vehicles.

There is also a so-called "chaotic rhythm" which, combined with inharmonious notes, multiplies imperil. Certain birds stimulate irritation and imperil through their voices, whereas others highly charge the atmosphere with bliss.

Cabbage, asparagus, celery, alcohol, drugs, and meat nourish imperil. These foods must be avoided when a group intends to perform rhythmic chanting, movements or dance.

> *Vexation is the plague of the World. It reacts upon the liver, and engenders certain bacilli which spread in a highly contagious action. The Emperor Akbar, upon sensing vexation in someone, would summon musicians so that a new rhythm would break up the infection. This action, even though physical, brought beneficial results.*
> Agni Yoga Society, *Fiery World, Vol. II*, para 165.

Vexation has a very close affinity with irritation. Vexation is the door to irritation. It starts in the emotional body, spreads into the mental body, descends into the nerves, and changes into irritation.

In Eastern countries, to prevent vexation in people who were wounded, or passing through light surgery and ordered to stay in bed for a few days, music and dances were presented, or great storytellers were invited to tell interesting stories. In this way joy was kept alive and vexation was repelled. Vexation also brings bitterness, irritation, and imperil. Imperil combined with the bacilli of vexation creates degenerative diseases in many organs, strongly affecting the liver.

Imperil is also treated through certain shocks. If one is clairvoyant and can see or sense the area of accumulation of imperil, he can shock the person by suddenly hitting the area in such a way that all his electrical fires focus for one instant at the point of contact. Such a focus of fires destroys and cleans the imperil.

There are other dangerous methods to shock people to restore their sight and remove paralysis, but such methods must be used only by those who know how to apply them in the right way with sufficient experience.

> *Often accidental shocks restore sight, hearing, and other lost senses. Does not this force one to think the crystal of imperil and other sediments have been suddenly expelled from the organism? Thus, strive to understand why sometimes in antiquity shock was applied in treatment of certain illnesses and paralysis.*
> Agni Yoga Society, *Fiery World, Vol. II*, para. 387.

We know about ulcers, but there are also ulcers that appear in our astral body. These ulcers are produced by imperil and low desires. Nature tries to heal these ulcers from the subtle bodies by throwing them out through the physical body. Most of the physical illnesses are the purifications of the subtle bodies. The illnesses of subtle bodies must manifest through the physical body in order to be cured in the subtle bodies.

The ulcers of the subtle bodies

> . . . *are carried over into the Subtle World if they are not gotten rid of on the Earth. Liberation from the physical vehicle does not mean deliverance from spiritual ulcers.* . . .
> Agni Yoga Society, *Fiery World, Vol. III*, para. 103.

> . . . *blots, noticeable on the aura, must be studied as indexes of various spiritual ulcers.* . . .
> Agni Yoga Society, *Fiery World, Vol. III*, para. 159.

> *Worry is a chasm of misery. He who gives himself up to worry is like a man in a burning house. Waves of flame almost consume him. He is full of a desire only to escape from the house. Scraps of thought are tossing about and fill him with irritation. In this chaos fear is born, and the will becomes paralyzed. Hence one must avoid worry. Yet calmness is not absence of feeling nor inaction.*
> Agni Yoga Society, *Fiery World, Vol. III*, para. 588.

There was a beautiful song which people in the Far East used to sing at the time of grief to find comfort. It was:

> *I do not fill my heart with worry.*
> *I do not worry for the things in the past,*
>   *because I cannot change them.*
> *I do not worry for the things in the present,*
>   *because I can deal with them.*
> *I do not worry about things in the future,*
>   *because I know the future always will be beautiful, if I walk on the right path toward my vision.*

Worry is dispersed by analysis and planning in the right direction, and then by raising our consciousness to a higher level. We are told that worry dwells in the lower mental planes and creates whirlpools there in which a man is caught. Expansion of consciousness toward the stars and toward Infinity breaks the spell of worry and sets the person free. Some people invoke the light of their Soul. Some invoke the light of Christ. Some enter into deep meditation and contact the Core of their being. These are techniques to be used at the slightest attack of worry.

At the time of World War II when times were dark, the Tibetan Master constantly used to repeat, "The Hierarchy stands, and Christ is closer to humanity than ever before."

> *... The defeat of falsehood must take place by the raising of the Fiery Sword, but not through irritation.*
> Agni Yoga Society, *Aum*, para. 66.

The fiery sword is often the symbol of decisive action with power of the will and clear vision. Irritation leads to wrong action, to emotional and egotistic involvements. Raising of the fiery sword is the action of a mighty warrior, when the lightning of the spirit is operating in its full power.

> *... Light does not coalesce with irritation and fear.*
> Agni Yoga Society, *Aum*, para. 144.

> *... Irritation is a poor conductor.*
> Agni Yoga Society, *Aum*, para. 206.

If the precipitates of space upon cities were to be investigated, something similar to imperil would be found among the poisonous substances. Carefully observing this poison, one comes to the conviction that it is imperil exhaled by the breath of evil. Undoubtedly, breathing permeated with evil is a carrier of injurious effects. If poison can be deposited in the organism, due to irritation, if the saliva can be made poisonous, then the breath can also be made a poison-carrier. It is necessary to judge how much evil is being exhaled and how multiform are the aspects of evil compressed in the new combinations of poisons present in enormous crowds of people. This is increased by the varied effluvia of decomposing foods and all manner of refuse which litter the streets even in metropolises. It is time to look after the cleanliness of backyards. Cleanliness is necessary out of doors and in the human breathing. The imperil exhaled by irritated people is identical with filth, or shameful refuse. It is imperative to impress people's consciousness with the fact that each bit of filth infects those around. The filth of moral dissolution is worse than any excretions.

Agni Yoga Society, *Aum*, para. 293.

Nothing can vindicate the self-generation of poison, it is the equivalent of murder and suicide. Even the most undeveloped people sense the approach of such a poison-bearer. Distress, anxiety and fear enter with him. Many physical diseases break out as a result of the infiltration of imperil — just as if a firebrand had worked its way in.

Agni Yoga Society, *Aum*, para. 294.

I remember one day when my father, talking about genocide, said, "We knew about their plans. Their whole being was engulfed by irritation. One could almost feel the poison they had in their livers. The rattlesnake could no longer bear the pressure of the accumulated poison; a victim had to be found."

When I was studying the psychology of genocide, I saw clearly what my father indicated. There was a planned, systematic injection of irritation into the veins of leadership which produced abundant imperil. This imperil not only urged them to genocide, but also obscured the light of their consciousness and the light of their Souls. It is observed that when they reached the end of their destructive deeds, the leadership and the nation collapsed.

When the leadership loses serenity and common sense, and is caught in the flame of hatred, anger, revenge, and irritation, one can clearly see the downfall of a nation or a group of nations.

It is very probable that before a criminal is produced, irritation is first injected into him by dark forces. After he is caught in irritation, anger, and revenge, the imperil will grow abundantly and he will not hesitate to commit crimes.

In the city where I was raised, there was a very dignified judge, full of wisdom and courage. One day, speaking with my father, he said, "I cannot run my office until I get rid of all those who are irritable or have irritation. I even can sense negativity and its emanating odor in my office." Later I asked father what irritation was. He answered, "Irritation is like termites. It kills life and prevents clear thinking or clear observation."

> *In anger and irritation man considers himself strong — this is according to earthly considerations. But regarded from the Subtle World, the irritated man is especially powerless. He attracts to himself a great number of small entities which*

> *feed on the emanations of anger. Besides, he lets down his own bars and allows even the lower beings to read his thoughts. Therefore, the state of irritation is inadmissible not only as a producer of imperil but also as a gateway for lower entities.*
>
> *Certainly each irritated person readily agrees with this explanation, but he immediately succumbs to still greater irritation — such is the nature of the ordinary human being. It is amazing how easily they agree, only the more easily to yield again. For this they will invent extraordinary justifications. It may be that the Higher World itself seems guilty in the disordered consciousness of the superficial earth-dweller! It is astonishing to observe people placing the blame for all their own offenses on the Higher World!*
>
> *Thus one can see that the simplest truths are in need of constant repetition.*
>
> Agni Yoga Society, ***Aum***, para. 331.

We are told that many emotions or feelings cannot be identified by names or words. They appear similar, such as indignation and irritation, shock and fear, and so on, but they can be differentiated by their sediments.

M.M. says that

> *. . . the time will come when science will discover the means of analyzing the substance secreted during each emotion. . . .*
>
> Agni Yoga Society, ***Aum***, para. 333.

> *. . . An investigator must not be irritated or agitated during observations. The manifestation of calmness will be a sign of Service. It is impossible to be devoted to Service if one's essence be*

billowing like waves under a cross wind.
Agni Yoga Society, ***Brotherhood***, para. 30.

No one can hit the target if his hands are shaking. Irritation disturbs the focus of consciousness, and the observing eye fluctuates. It prevents the flow of love which makes a person understand. Irritation creates repulsion and obscures the radiation of service. Our social service will greatly improve when we act under the impulse to serve without the imperil of irritation, repulsion, pressure, and hate.

. . . The symphony of qualities is like the symphony of the spheres. If one quality develops beautifully while others are straggling, there results a destructive dissonance. Dissonance can be weakening or irritating, or even destructive. Equilibrium of qualities is achieved through great tension of consciousness. The shepherd must carefully tend his flock, and likewise must man cure an ailing quality.
Agni Yoga Society, ***Brotherhood***, para. 60.

Children attract irritation quickly, and if it is continuous, it creates destruction in their lives. That is why teachers are selected very carefully in certain communities. The future of a child is in the hands of the teacher. If the teacher is irritable or full of imperil, his students will have a hard time cleaning themselves from the effects of irritation and imperil.

The threatening time is very near. Do not the heat-lightnings already flash out, and are not the ominous messengers of the awakened subterranean fire breaking through? We who know about it must urgently transmute our inner fires in order to assimilate the approaching fiery

storm, as only this will give a stability in the battle, will bring us near the Hierarchy of Light, and will help to fill the chalice. Thus, let us transmute all our energies. We should start from the most stubborn energy, which is egoism (that furious dragon of selfishness with its long tail); self-conceit; love of power; self-love; touchiness; irritability; fear; doubt and other similar decorations. And we should replace them with the wings of affirmed unity; complete solidarity with all the co-workers; acknowledgement of Hierarchy; joyous strengthening of the given tasks; tolerance and gratitude for the right directions. We should conclude with — trust to the very end. All this transmutation is so simplified when hearts burn with devotion and love to the One who calls to construction and who points out the way to the Tower.
Agni Yoga Society, Letters of Helena Roerich, Vol.I, pp. 24-25.

For the last time I shall speak of irritation. Discern its harm — not only personal, but also for space. This worm, concealed by a smile and politeness, does not cease to devour the aura. Its harm creeps beneath all works.

For the sake of creation, be permeated with the conviction against irritation. When, as a bloody clot, it closes the ear, can a man hear? When the eye is clouded, can the man see? When the curtain falls on the consciousness, where then is acquisition?
Agni Yoga Society, Agni Yoga, para. 369.

Index

Aeroperil •13
Agni •51
Air •37
Alcohol •52
Analysis •27, 55
Anger •7, 18, 57
Apathy •6
Appreciation •9, 32
Art imitation of•46
Articles [contaminated]•14-15
Attitude(s) •26, 27
Aura •6, 9, 10, 14, 18, 24, 28, 29, 31, 33, 34-35, 54
Balance •24, 39
Barley •29, 31
Beauty •21, 24-25, 26-27, 29, 32-33, 34, 39, 46
Betrayal •45
Bitterness •53
Bliss •15, 17, 24, 35, 36, 52
Body(ies)
    astral •6, 7, 9, 10-11, 28, 29, 32, 38, 45, 48, 51
    etheric •6, 10, 14, 35-36, 39
    PEM •28, 38, 53
    physical •7, 12, 35-36
    subtle •6, 10, 11, 22, 23, 28, 52, 53-54
Brain •47, 48
Breakdowns nervous•29
Cancer •6
Cells •6, 22, 28
Center(s) •6, 7, 11, 25, 27-28, 34, 35, 39, 48, 52
    astral•28
    nerve •49, 50
    solar plexus •6, 7, 12, 42
Channels nerve •12, 28, 39-40, 50
Chanting •10, 52
Child(ren) •11, 26, 39, 42, 59
Christ •36, 49 55
Colds •14
Colors •11
Coma •28
Compassion •23-24, 35
Complain(ing) •5, 8
Complex inferiority, •10, 5
Condemnation •11
Confusion •22, 36, 48
Consciousness •6, 8, 21, 30, 32, 42, 55, 57, 59
Contemplation •36, 43
Contentment •30, 37, 39
Control self-•40
Courage •24, 57
Cracks •21, 29
Creativity •37, 43, 45-46
Crime •11, 29
Criticism •5, 9, 34
Dance rhythmic•51-53
Daring •24, 30, 43
Deception •5, 8
Def. of
    analysis•27

Def. of (continued)
    contentment•37
    creativity•46
    disorderly thinking•48
    doubt•22
    frustration•24-25
    happiness•38
    harmlessness•33
    heart•35
    humility•43
    intolerance•10
    irritation•22
    joy•38
    patience•40
    proper sleep•38-39
    psychic energy•34
    resistance•23
    rest•39
    self-forgetfulness•33
    self-pity•22
    self-sacrifice•32-33
    sense of failure•24-25
    solemnity•44-45
    solitude•21
    tension•49
Defeat self- •49
Denial self- •22
Depression •7, 27-29, 41
Desires •7, 53
Detachment •27
Disease(s) •5, 6, 7, 9, 11, 53
Dislike •5, 7
Divorce •11
Doubt •10, 21, 22, 47
Drugs •10, 46, 48, 52
Ears •7, 11, 23
Electricity •6, 28, 35
Emotions •15, 27, 29, 33, 37, 38
Encouragement •9
Energy(ies) •6, 37, 39-40, 48, 49, 51-52
    bliss•15
    desire-•14
    healing•9, 50
    of Great Ones•34, 35
    psychic •9, 28, 34, 35, 37, 43, 44, 45, 51, 52
Enlightenment •15
Equilibrium •39, 51
Evil •43, 50, 51, 55-56
Exertion •35
    self- •49
Exploitation •8
Eye(s) •7, 14, 23, 50, 59
Fanaticism •26
Fear(s) •7, 10, 25, 43-44, 47, 55, 58
Forgetfulness self- •30, 33
Foundation •48
Freedom •8, 26-27
Freesias •29, 31
Frustration •10, 24-25, 40
Future •8, 24, 40, 44. 59
Genocide •56-57
Germs •6, 7, 18, 38
Givingness •9
Glamors •17
Glands •6, 34, 37, 52
Goodness •32-33, 39, 46
Gossip •5, 9, 34

Gratitude •9
Greed •11
Habit(s) •19, 40
Happiness •8, 30, 37, 38
Harmlessness •30, 33-34, 39
Harmony •39, 40
Hatred •5, 7, 47, 57, 59
Health •9, 12, 19, 38
Heart •6, 9, 12, 30, 35-36, 38, 44, 45, 49
Hierarchy •11, 30, 35, 46, 48, 55
Humanity •29, 46
Humility •30, 43
Hurry •5, 10
Hypnosis •25-26
Illnesses •11, 53-54
Illusions •17
Imbalance •29
Impatience •5, 10, 42
Imperil •6, 7, 9, 10, 11, 12, 13, 14, 15, 17, 18,19, 24, 25, 26, 27-28, 29, 31, 32, 33, 34, 37, 38, 39-40, 46, 47, 48, 50, 51, 52, 53, 55-56, 57, 59
    in
        astral and mental plane•18, 20, 25
        etheric body and aura•14
        food and water•14
        global aura•29
        group gatherings•46-47
        nerve channels•12
        objects and clothing•14-15
        public officials•15
        [public places]•15
        receptive apparatus•46
    rela. to
        genocide•57
        close contact with people•15
        compassion•35
        daring•43-44
        deception•8
        depression•27
        evil eye•14
        exertion•35
        exploitation•8
        freesias•31
        heavy labor•37
        impatience•42
        joy•31
        music and [narcotics]•46
        musk•31
        noise•11-12
        posthypnotic suggestion•25-26
        prayer•35-36
        psychic energy•9
        rhythm•52
        roses•30-31
        shocks•53
        sleeping under stars•43
        "White Forces"•46
Inclusiveness •9
Indifference •33-34, 45
Indignation •58
Inertia •39
Infinity •40, 42, 55
Ingratitude •5, 9
Insanity •29
Insomnia •29
Intercourse •14

Interest(s) •5
    of lower centers•7
    separative, prevention of•42
    self-, as widespread disease•9, 33
Intolerance •5, 10
Intuition •28
Irritation •5-6, 7, 9, 10, 12, 13, 14, 15-16, 17,18, 20, 21, 22, 23, 24, 26, 27, 29, 32, 33, 34, 35, 37, 38, 40, 43, 44, 45, 46, 47, 48, 49, 50, 52-53, 55, 57, 59, 60
    rela. to
        anger•18
        compassion•35
        creativity•45-46
        daring•43-44
        deception•8
        exploitation•8
        happiness•38
        heart•49
        impatience•42
        isolation•47
        love and tenderness•25
        music and [narcotics]•46
        noise•11-12
        orderliness•40
        patience•40
        posthypnotic suggestion•25-26
        prayer•36
        [psychic energy] on film•45
        revenge•8
        rhythm•52
        self-forgetfulness•33
        separatism•42-43
        service•59
        sleep•39
        Teaching•24
        understanding•59
        wasting energy•40
Isolation •7, 47
Joy •8, 24, 26-27, 29, 31, 32, 35, 38, 39, 41, 53
Kissing •14
Labor •30, 37, 49
Leadership •47, 57
Liver •53
Lotus •48
Love •24, 25, 29, 32, 39, 41, 59
Lungs •31
Magnanimity •51
Magnetism •7, 8-9
Marijuana •46
Master •21, 44
Meditation •18, 36, 43, 48, 55
Microbes •6
Mind •12, 21-22, 26, 30, 36, 37, 38, 39, 48
Mother •39
Movement(s) rhythmic•51-52
Movie(s) •7, 46
Music •10-11, 46, 51, 53
Musk •29, 31
Nadis •28
Nation(s) •51, 57
Negativity •9, 29
Nerves •31, 34, 52
Nirvana •36
Noise •6, 11, 12
Nose •7

Nourishment •30, 38
Observation(s) •9, 27, 58-59
Order(liness) •30, 40
Organs •6, 7, 12, 37, 42, 53
Pain •26
Paralysis •11, 53
Patience •23-24, 30, 40, 41, 42, 51
Peace •35, 37
Personality •7, 9, 38, 42, 47
Perspiration •12
Pity self- •21, 22
Plane(s) •15, 20, 24, 28, 29, 35-36, 43, 51, 52
Planning •55
Poison
  in
    aura, rela. to cracks•21
    solar plexus area•6
    space from [negative] thoughts•20
  of
    aeroperil•13
    destruction•8
    food while irritated•18
    imperil, spread of•6
    irritation•7
    revenge•8
    speech and words•17
    thoughts•18
    ungrateful people•9
Prana •34, 37
Prayer(s) •30, 18, 35-36
Prejudice •5, 7-8
Pride •33
Prisons •15
Problems
  health, rela. to complaining•9
  psychological, caused from noise•11
  psychological, from moving•16
  when electrical system is cut•6
Purity •39
Quarreling •5, 17, 37
Quote(s)
  AY•8, 11, 13, 18, 17, 19, 20-21, 38, 40-41, 44, 45, 46, 47, 49, 50, 51, 52,53, 54, 55, 56, 57-59, 60
  Christ•18, 22
  The Bhagavad Gita•49
  Tibetan Master•55
  TS father•56-57
Rays •43
Reaction •5, 8
Reasoning •24
Rejection •5, 7, 23
Repulsion •59
Resentment •5
Resistance •23-24, 33
Rest •30, 38, 39
Reticence •41
Revenge •57
Rhythm(s) •39, 51, 52
Roses •29, 30-31
Sacrifice self- •30, 32-33
Sanctuary •14
Satisfaction self- •5, 9
Sattva •52
Sediment •22-23
Self •21, 22, 30, 33, 36, 43
Separatism •29, 42

Serenity •36, 37, 41, 47, 57
Sex •10
Shock(s) •53, 58
Sickness •10
Sight •50, 53
Silence •12, 18, 41, 47
Singing •51, 52
Skin •15
Sleep •30, 35, 38, 39
Solemnity •24, 30, 44-45, 51
Solitude •21
Soul •9, 25-26, 28, 34, 35, 38, 44, 55, 57
Sound •23
Space •13-14, 17, 18, 21
Speech •17
Stability •24
Stars •30, 43, 55
Story of
  boy throwing rock at window•33-34
  eating while irritated•19
  holy man who lived in house•16
  Socrates, rela. to serenity•22
  used sofa•16-17
Storytellers •53
Striving •8, 35, 39, 44
Suffering •26, 43
Suggestions posthypnotic•25-26
Suicide •11
Superstition •16, 26
System
  digestive•6
  mental•11
  nervous •6-7, 10, 22, 23, 27, 28, 29, 31, 34, 35, 37, 40, 43, 52
Teacher(s) •21, 34, 59
Teaching •12, 17, 30, 34, 41, 48, 49
Temper •5, 7
Tenderness •25
Tension •10, 39, 49
Thinking •11, 12, 38, 47, 48
Thought •5, 8, 15, 17, 18, 19, 20, 21, 31, 33, 34, 47, 48
Time •21
Tissues •35, 37
Touch •14
Triad Spiritual•36
Truth •32-33, 39, 46
Tumors •6, 28-29
Ulcers •53, 54
Understanding •6-7, 9, 23-24, 39, 59
Urges •25, 29
Vexation •41, 52, 53
Virtues •34
Vision(s) •7, 18, 34, 40, 43, 45, 55
Vitality •7, 14
Water •14, 15, 37
Web etheric•21
Whirlpools •28-29, 55
Will •9-10, 26, 55
Wisdom •9, 12, 24-25, 43
Wormwood oil or tea •29, 31
Worry •7, 54, 55

Write to the Aquarian Educational Group for additional information regarding:

- Free catalog of author's books and music tapes
- Information regarding lecture tapes and videos
- Placement on mailing list
- Information on new releases
- Torkom Saraydarian's book called *The Psyche and Psychism*, in which part of this book is a chapter

A Daily Discipline of Worship	$2.00	_____
Earthquakes and Disasters	$5.00	_____
Fiery Carriage and Drugs	$3.00	_____
Five Great Mantrams of the New Age	$2.50	_____
Hierarchy and the Plan	$2.00	_____
Irritation — The Destructive Fire	$5.00	_____
Questioning Traveler and Karma	$2.50	_____
Synthesis	$2.50	_____
Torchbearers	$2.50	_____
The Unusual Court	$5.00	_____

Total for book(s) _____
AZ Residents add 7% sales tax _____
Subtotal _____

    Postage, Insurance and Handling:
      (in U.S.A. — Please write us for overseas charges.)

Amount of Order	**Charge**
$2.00 - $5.00	$1.75
$5.01 - $15.00	$2.25
$15.01 - $25.00	$3.75

    For orders over $25.00, the charge is
    $3.50 plus $0.50 for each additional $5.00.

Postage and Handling _____
Total Money Order Enclosed _____

NAME_____

ADDRESS_____

CITY,STATE,ZIP_____

BOOKS ARE NOT RETURNABLE • PAYABLE IN UNITED STATES FUNDS
Make Money Order payable to:
Aquarian Educational Group
P.O. Box 267, Sedona, AZ 86336